# JAMES MONROE

By Linda Wade

Illustrated by
Karen Neulinger

Acknowledgement: Special thanks to James Wooton, Curator of Ash Lawn-Highland, located near Charlottesville, Virginia.


Library of Congress Catalog Card No. 92-074518
Printed in the United States of America
ISBN 0-87386-088-8 (Paperback Edition)
ISBN 0-87386-089-6 (Library Edition)

# JAMES MONROE

James Monroe, fifth President of the United States, was the fourth President born in Virginia! He was born in Westmoreland County on April 28, 1758. His parents were Spence and Elizabeth Jones Monroe. Mr. Monroe came from a Scottish family that had settled in Virginia in the mid-1600's. Mrs. Monroe's family had come to Virginia from Wales. They, too, had been in America for many years. James was the second-oldest of four boys and a girl. Their home was a small farm on Monroe Creek.

James studied at home with a tutor until he was about twelve years old. Then he went to Parson Campbell's school, some distance away. It was at this school that James met and became friends with John Marshall, who would later become chief justice of the United States. Every day James left his home early in the morning with his rifle. He carried it not only for protection, but also to shoot game as he returned home.

At the age of sixteen, James entered the College of William and Mary in Williamsburg, Virginia. Williamsburg was the capital of colonial Virginia and a center of revolutionary talk and action! Many of the college students at William and Mary became involved in political activities. James Monroe was one of those students!

James was so filled with patriotism that early in 1776 he dropped out of William and Mary College. He left his books and became a soldier under General George Washington. He fought in the battles at Harlem Heights and White Plains in the fall of 1776. On Christmas Eve, Lieutenant Monroe was among the first of Washington's troops to cross the half-frozen Delaware River. They surprised the British Hessians at Trenton. It was at the Battle of Trenton that Monroe was severely wounded in the shoulder. His superior officers praised his bravery, and General Washington promoted him to captain. During the next two years, Monroe took part in the battles at Brandywine Creek, Germantown, and Monmouth.

In 1778 Monroe was promoted to lieutenant colonel and sent to raise troops in Virginia. Unfortunately, he was unable to raise such a regiment. But he did get to know the governor of

Virginia—Thomas Jefferson. It was the beginning of a life-long friendship, even though Jefferson was fifteen years older than Monroe. The two were also very close friends with another Virginian—James Madison. The three Virginians held many of the same political beliefs and ideals. Their political careers would follow very similar paths!

At the end of the war James decided to remain in Williamsburg to study law under Jefferson. When the capital moved to Richmond, Monroe followed Jefferson there.

James Monroe's political career began in 1782 when he was only 24 years old. He was elected to the Virginia General Assembly. A year later he was elected to the Fourth Congress of the Confederation. He served there for three years. Monroe favored westward expansion. He worked hard to give pioneers the right to travel on the Mississippi River. He also helped Jefferson draft laws for the development of the West.

In 1786 the tall, blue-eyed Virginian married 17-year-old Elizabeth Kortright. James and Elizabeth were happy together. In time, they had two daughters and a son. Sadly, the boy died at only eighteen months of age.

In October 1786 James set up a law practice in Fredericksburg, Virginia. But he was still interested in a career in politics. In 1787 Monroe was chosen as a member of the Virginia House of Delegates. In 1788 a state convention was called to ratify the United States Constitution. James Monroe was elected as a delegate to that convention. His distrust of a strong central government put him on the opposing side, along with Patrick Henry. But Monroe did not offer great opposition and accepted the Constitution once it was ratified. It did bother him that there was no bill of rights, but he felt sure that one would be added.

In 1789 the Monroes decided to build a plantation near Jefferson's home in Monticello. The Monroes admired Thomas Jefferson not only for his political ideas, but also for his creative abilities. Jefferson was a capable architect. They asked Jefferson to help plan their new farm. Called Highland because it stood high on a mountain, they were able to look out to the Blue Ridge Mountains from their new home.

With the ratification of the Constitution, 1789 brought about some changes in the government. George Washington was chosen to become the first President of the United States of America. Monroe lost to James Madison when he tried to become a member of the first United States House of Representatives. A year later, however, the Virginia legislature elected him to fill a vacancy in the United States Senate.

During this term, Monroe sided with Jefferson and Madison against Secretary of the Treasury Alexander Hamilton. Hamilton's party became known as the Federalist Party. The party led by Jefferson and Madison was called the Democratic-Republican Party; although it was often called the Republican Party, its policies were really more like the modern Democratic Party.

In 1794, President Washington appointed James Monroe Minister to France. Monroe did not agree with all of Washington's policies, but

Washington knew that James understood and admired the French people. He felt that Monroe could improve political relations between the two countries. At that time the new French government was at war with Great Britain. The United States recognized the new French government, but was determined to remain neutral and at peace. Both sides made neutrality difficult.

President Washington sent John Jay to England to negotiate a treaty. The agreement that resulted was called Jay's Treaty. Monroe criticized it as being too weak. He said that it unfairly favored the British. Washington was annoyed that Monroe did not do more to defend the treaty to the French. He felt that Monroe's remarks against the treaty were disloyal. He also felt that Monroe had too much sympathy for the French revolutionists. By the end of 1796 Monroe was called home, angry and humiliated.

In 1797 an ongoing feud between James Monroe and Alexander Hamilton became public. Hamilton believed that Monroe had been responsible for the release of scandalous information about him. Monroe denied that he was to blame. A duel nearly resulted. These were not happy years for James Monroe.

Despite these embarrassments, James Monroe remained popular with the people. In 1799 he was appointed governor of Virginia; he held the position for three years.

His old friend Thomas Jefferson became President in 1801. Jefferson knew of Monroe's ability to communicate with the French; therefore, he sent him to Paris in 1803. Monroe's mission was to help Robert R. Livingston negotiate the purchase of New Orleans.

Monroe was in for quite a surprise. Napoleon needed money to fight his impending war with England. He offered to sell to the United States the entire province of Louisiana. Monroe and Livingston made the Louisiana Purchase for 15 million dollars—less than 3 cents an acre! The huge purchase doubled the size of the United States! It stretched from the Gulf of Mexico to the Canadian border and covered 827,987 square miles. The western boundary moved from the Mississippi River to the Rocky Mountains.

Although hailed a hero by many for the Louisiana Purchase, more hard times lay ahead for James Monroe. From Paris, Monroe went to London as Minister to England. He tried to negotiate a shipping treaty, but he was not successful.

President Jefferson then sent him to Madrid. He was to help Charles Pinckney convince Spain to give up or sell West Florida. This area had not been included in the Louisiana Purchase. They could not get Spain to agree.

Once again Monroe left for London. This time he and William Pinkney were to secure a trade treaty with Great Britain. Most important to President Jefferson was the impressment of American seamen by the British. The British had insisted on the right to board American ships in search of British deserters. It was hard to tell the British from the Americans. They often removed

American seamen and impressed them into the British navy!

Monroe and Pinkney did negotiate a treaty. But it said nothing about the impressment of American seamen. The treaty was so unsatisfactory to President Jefferson that he didn't even submit it to the Senate! In 1807 Monroe returned home.

Shortly after his arrival, Monroe found himself a reluctant candidate for the presidential nomination. His opponent was his long-time friend James Madison. Madison won the nomination—and the election—overwhelmingly.

Monroe felt hurt when Madison did not appoint him to his cabinet as secretary of state. Madison did offer him the governorship of Louisiana, but Monroe refused. If he wasn't going to be secretary of state, he would prefer an elected office.

James Monroe was elected to the Virginia Assembly in 1810. After serving there a few months, he once again was chosen governor of Virginia. He held that office, too, only a short time. Three months after President Madison took office, he asked James to serve as secretary of state. James accepted.

Monroe would have the difficult task of trying to arrive at a conciliation with Great Britain and France. France and Britain were at war. Neither country would honor the neutrality that the United States wished to uphold. War with Britain loomed on the horizon. American sailors continued to be taken by the British. The British held to their claim that the men they took were deserters from the Royal Navy.

On June 16, 1812, Congress declared war on Great Britain. Ironically, only two days earlier Great Britain had agreed to the terms asked by the United States. Poor communications prevented this fact from reaching President Madison until the fighting was underway!

Being a former military man, Monroe was eager to take command of the army. Madison wanted him to remain secretary of state. After the burning of Washington by the British, however, Madison became convinced that Secretary of War John Armstrong had neglected his duties. He asked Monroe to take on the additional post of secretary of war. Monroe held both posts for the rest of the war. The War of 1812 ended with neither side really being able to claim victory; nevertheless, James Monroe's efforts as secretary of war made him known throughout the nation!

As President Madison's second term was nearing its end, it seemed only natural that Monroe would run for office. He won easily, defeating the Federalist candidate, Senator Rufus King, by 183 to 34 electoral votes. On March 4, 1817, at 58 years of age, James Monroe became the fifth President of the United States. His boyhood friend John Marshall, now chief justice and with different political views, administered the oath of office.

The President's House had not yet been rebuilt after being burned by the British. The Monroes moved into a nearby home; they lived there for nine months. Part of this time was spent on a good-will trip. James Monroe wanted to meet the people of the United States. Shortly after taking office he began his travels throughout New England and as far west as Detroit. Everywhere he went he was met by excited crowds. This was the first time many people had ever seen a President; they cheered him at every stop.

A reporter for a Boston newspaper called this the "era of good feeling." The name stuck. Although things would not always be perfect, Monroe's terms in office were basically calm and prosperous. His presidency came to be known as the Era of Good Feeling.

For the most part, the name seemed to fit the mood of the entire nation. When the War of 1812 had begun, Americans were importing most of their goods. As the war progressed, Americans produced more and more for themselves. While most people still farmed for a living, new industries were founded. Cities grew. Philadelphia even had paved streets and a city water system. Many Americans moved west; land was cheap and the spirit of adventure was high. Opportunities were limitless.

While President Monroe was meeting the people of the nation, workers were busy repairing the President's House. A heavy coat of white paint was applied to cover the damage. Upon Monroe's return to Washington in September 1817, the President's House—soon to be called the White House—was ready for occupancy!

President Monroe had been impressed by European formality. He insisted that the White House be run in a formal manner. The Monroes adopted a strict social code. Those who wished to see the President had to be invited or had to make an appointment. While this caused some Americans to feel shut out, it brought about a closer relationship with many foreign leaders.

The Monroes decided to build a home closer to Washington. James had inherited property and a house in Loudoun County, Virginia. He asked Thomas Jefferson to help draw up plans to replace that house with a more spacious one. The new house would have a wide portico with 30-foot columns. It was set on a sloping lawn surrounded by a grove of oak trees. Monroe called this stately mansion Oak Hill.

James Monroe was a popular President. He had strong, stable advisors. He was careful to avoid sectional favoritism in his choice of cabinet members. John Quincy Adams of Massachusetts was appointed secretary of state. John Calhoun of South Carolina was made secretary of war. He appointed his rival for the election, William Crawford of Georgia, secretary of the treasury. Americans were pleased with these choices.

An important issue of Monroe's first term was called the American System. Congress wanted to strengthen the country faster by building new roads and canals to open up the West. This would also help manufacturers of the northern states develop American markets. Monroe opposed this system. Although he believed that these roads and canals were important, he did not think that Congress had the constitutional right to build them. Monroe vetoed the bill. The second part of the American System was more successful. It had to do with tariffs. In April 1818 a bill to increase the duty on iron products was passed.

Monroe's first term also saw a crisis in the banking industry. This crisis is known as the Panic of 1819. The banks had been loaning money too freely. Finally, the directors of the

United States Bank ordered their branches not to renew any personal mortgages. They also ordered them to present all of their state bank notes to the state banks for immediate payment. The state banks were unable to meet this obligation. State banks crashed one after another. The South was especially hard hit. President Monroe visited those states to try to calm the rising tide of sectionalism.

Many blamed the national bank and called for the repeal of its charter. President Monroe preferred to reform it. The president of the bank and its board of directors were forced to resign. President Monroe convinced Langdon Cheves of South Carolina to take over as president of the bank. Cheves was known for his outstanding financial ability. It would be quite a while before all was well, but the national bank was saved.

There was another issue that added to the rise of sectionalism. Many northerners were expressing the opinion that slavery was morally wrong. This issue was brought to a head when Missouri applied for admission to the Union as a slave state.

After much debate, a compromise finally was reached. The Missouri Compromise admitted Missouri as a slave state and Maine as a free state. There would be 12 free states and 12 slave states. The North and the South would each have 24 senators. Although slavery would be permitted in Missouri, it would be banned from the rest of the Louisiana Territory north of latitude $36^0$ 30’. This became known as the Mason-Dixon Line. Already the nation was beginning the struggle that would culminate in the Civil War.

Another problem during Monroe's first term had to do with the Seminole Indians in Florida. They often raided the Georgia farms, stealing the cattle and sometimes killing the families. They then escaped into East Florida, which was still owned by Spain.

Acting on his own, Major General Andrew Jackson chased a group of marauding Seminoles into East Florida. He defeated the Seminoles and captured the Spanish fort of Saint Marks. Two British subjects captured there were hanged. A court martial had found them guilty of spying and of inciting the Indians against the Americans. Jackson then marched to Pensacola and captured it, too. Both Spain and England were angered by these occurrences. But Spain realized that it could not defend Florida properly. In 1819 Spain agreed to give Florida to the United States in return for the cancellation of five million dollars in American claims.

When President Monroe ran for a second term, only one electoral vote was cast against him. One elector cast a ballot for John Quincy Adams; George Washington remained the only President to be elected unanimously by the Electoral College.

During Monroe's administration, the nation grew and prospered. Five new states were added: Mississippi, Illinois, Alabama, Maine, and Missouri. President Monroe also continued his successful foreign policy by securing peaceful boundaries with Canada.

But his greatest success came near the end of his second term. It came in the form of a policy that would later become known as the Monroe Doctrine. The Monroe Doctrine became the basic policy of United States international relations. It is still in effect today.

The policy came about because several Latin American countries had just declared their independence from Spain. Monroe feared that European powers might try to gain control over some of the weaker countries. He knew that Spain had asked the help of France in reconquering the newly freed countries.

In his annual message to Congress on December 2, 1823, President Monroe made it clear that the United States did not want European countries to meddle in American affairs. He stated that "we should consider any attempt on their part to extend their system to any portion of this hemisphere as dangerous to our peace and safety." He also said that there could be no new colonies started in the Americas. In other words, the United States would not permit foreign interference in the New World. At the same time, he assured the European nations that the United States would not interfere in Europe's political affairs.

In August 1824 President Monroe received a special honor. The capital city of Liberia was named Monrovia to thank him for his support. Liberia was in West Africa. It had been founded in 1817 to colonize the free Negroes from the United States. Although Monroe had been a slave owner himself, he did a great deal to help the American Colonization Society.

James Monroe left the White House after eight years. He retired to his home in Virginia. These later years were marred by financial difficulties. Much of his time was spent trying to collect money due him from the government. It was owed to him for expenses during his long career in public service.

But these years were not unhappy ones. It pleased him to resume his friendships with Thomas Jefferson and James Madison. In 1824 he followed in their footsteps by becoming regent of the University of Virginia. In 1826 he was saddened by Jefferson's death. But Madison and he were both on the committee to amend the state constitution in 1829.

When his wife died in 1830, James closed his beautiful home. He moved to New York City to live with one of his married daughters. He died there at the age of 73. It was July 4, 1831—five years to the day after the deaths of Thomas Jefferson and John Adams. The "Virginia Dynasty" had ended.